101 Uses for a JACK Russell